MYASIA WHITE

UNBREAKABLE

BENT BUT NOT BROKEN!

UNBREAKABLE
BENT BUT NOT BROKEN!

MYASIA WHITE

Book Cover Design: SHERO Publishing
Editing: Synergy Ed Consulting
Graphics & Design: Greenlight Consulting
Publishing: SHERO Publishing

UNBREAKABLE
BENT BUT NOT BROKEN!

TABLE OF CONTENT

Introduction

I am a survivor of unspeakable trauma. At 26 years old, I carry the weight of experiences that have shaped me in ways that I never could have imagined. From childhood age to teenage years old, I was a victim of molestation by someone I trusted wholeheartedly. The betrayal and violation of my innocence left scars that cut deep into my soul, shaping the person I have become.

Growing up without a father further compounded the challenges I faced. As I navigated the complexities of life without the presence of a paternal figure, the absence of a father's love and guidance left me vulnerable to the manipulations of others. This led to a cycle of narcissistic abuse from ages 17 to 21. All to experience single motherhood at the age of 19.

Through the darkness and pain, I have found strength and resilience within myself. This is how I turned my *test into testimonies* with God on my side to help change my story. This is my story of survival, healing, and the journey to reclaiming my voice and my power.

Welcome to ***Unbreakable: Bent But Not Broken.***

UNBREAKABLE
BENT BUT NOT BROKEN!

MYASIA WHITE

CHAPTER 1:
Born into a Story

Chapter 1:
Born into a Story

A Dramatic Arrival

I don't remember the day I was born. How could I? I was just a few hours old. Yet over the years, I've heard the story of that day so many times that it feels as though I was there, experiencing it myself. Like any birth, my arrival was marked by excitement, joy, and a touch of unpredictability. The way my mom and family tell it makes one thing clear: it was a day that changed everything.

It was January 8, 1999, around 1:00 p.m., when I entered the world. My mama, just 21 years old, was in her hospital room, watching *Days of Our Lives*. She always says she wasn't in much pain—nothing like what she'd imagined labor would be. The contractions weren't intense, and she felt so relaxed that she was more invested in the drama unfolding on TV than in her own delivery. She called it an easy birth.

Then, suddenly, it happened.

One minute, she was engrossed in the fictional lives of the characters in Salem, and the next, she felt an overwhelming, instinctual pressure. She turned to the nurse and casually said, "I think I need to poop." Whether it was her calm demeanor or sheer disbelief about how far along she was, she wasn't worried. The nurse came to check her, and everything changed instantly.

I was already halfway out.

What followed was a blur of urgency. There was no time for panic, no time to call family, and no time for questions. The doctors rushed in, and in what felt like the blink of an eye, I was born. It was as smooth as my mama had hoped for—no complications, no drama, just a small but healthy baby ready to start life.

My mama always says that the first time she held me was like holding a piece of heaven. She felt an overwhelming love—the kind only a mother can feel. Everything seemed perfect, like the start of a beautiful story. But little did anyone know; this was just the prologue to a much more dramatic chapter.

A Life-Threatening Challenge

The first ten days of my life passed uneventfully. My mama cared for me like any new mother would—loving, attentive, and protective. Then, on the tenth day, everything changed.

My cousin, just two years old at the time, came to visit. Like most toddlers, he was full of energy and curiosity, eager to meet the newest member of the family. It seemed like an innocent visit. No one could have predicted that this moment would set off a chain of events threatening my life.

I don't know when the symptoms first appeared, but my mama remembers it all too well. I began struggling to breathe. It wasn't the occasional ragged gasp of a newborn—it was deeper, more alarming. My tiny chest heaved with every breath, my face contorted in visible distress. My mama's heart sank as she watched me struggle, helpless and terrified.

She didn't wait. Without hesitation, she rushed me to the hospital. There, in a flurry of frantic activity, I was taken from her arms as nurses and doctors worked urgently to stabilize me. The diagnosis came quickly: bronchiolitis. It's a viral infection that inflames the small airways in the lungs. While common in young children, it can be deadly for a newborn. The doctors believed the virus had likely come from my cousin, who, like most toddlers, had no concept of how easily germs spread. For a baby as small and fragile as I was, the situation was critical.

The prognosis was grim. The doctors told my mama plainly: most newborns with severe bronchiolitis don't survive. My tiny lungs were fighting a battle they couldn't win alone.

Faith and a Miracle

Hearing those words shattered my mama. She had only just begun to experience the joy of motherhood, and now, she was faced with the possibility of losing me. Confused and heartbroken, she didn't know what to do.

But she did know who to call.

My grandparents arrived at the hospital as quickly as they could. When they saw me—tiny, frail, and struggling for every breath—they were shaken but not defeated. They believed in the power of prayer, and they weren't ready to give up on me.

My grandmother, the rock of our family, immediately began to pray. Then, in an act of faith and love, she started singing. It wasn't just any song—it was *This Old Man,* the nursery rhyme she had sung to me while I was still in the womb.

"This old man, he played one, He played knick-knack paddy whack, Give the dog a bone, This old man came rolling home…"

As her voice filled the sterile hospital room, my grandfather joined in, their voices rising together with a kind of unshakable belief only grandparents can have. My mama says that something shifted in that moment. The fear and heaviness that had consumed the room began to lift.

It wasn't just a lullaby. It was a declaration of faith, a battle cry for my life.

Within hours, something miraculous happened. The machines tracking my vitals showed improvement. My breathing stabilized, my color returned, and the doctors, once pessimistic, were amazed at my sudden recovery.

I survived.

In the days that followed, my family couldn't stop praising God for the miracle. My mama called me her "miracle baby." From that point on, I carried the story of survival—a testimony of faith, love, and resilience.

A Family's Journey

As I grew older, my mama would tell me this story often. She'd remind me that I had survived something many babies don't and that God must have a purpose for my life. I didn't yet know what that purpose was, but I lived each day believing in it.

Looking back, I see the contrast of where my family stood then and where we stand now. When I was born, my family was close-knit, always there for one another, and united in love. But over the years, things changed. Today, they are full of drama, competition, and distance. They support strangers before supporting each other and pick and choose who qualifies as "family."

My Mother's Strength

My mother's journey was equally complex. At 21, she already had one child and depended on her great-grandparents for stability. She wasn't prepared for motherhood and faced the harsh reality of figuring out her life. My paternity was uncertain at first, leading to DNA tests that confirmed my father's identity only when I was six years old. Even then, he chose to remain distant.

Through all of this, my mother endured and grew. She faced physical and emotional abuse, single motherhood, and financial struggles. But she remained resilient, ensuring my siblings and I never felt the weight of her burdens. She showed me what it meant to be a warrior. Today, she stands as a successful business owner with three strong, united children and two grandchildren.

Standing Tall

Hearing the stories about the day I was born and the battles I survived, I know my life was destined to be different. I've faced molestation, absent fatherhood, teenage pregnancy, and narcissistic abuse. But like my mother, I've stood tall. She showed me how to rise above, and I now stand as an independent woman, a business owner, and a published author. My daughter sees me as a true warrior, and she'll never know the struggles I endured.

From the moment I was born—surrounded by love, prayers, and hope—I was part of something much bigger than myself. I know that God has something greater in store for me, and that, I believe, is the greatest miracle of all.

"From the moment I was born—surrounded by love, prayers, and hope—I was part of something much bigger than myself. I don't yet know what that purpose is, but I live each day believing in it."

~Myasia White

CHAPTER 2:

The Missing Piece

Chapter 2:
The Missing Piece

A Void in Every Story

While growing up, I often heard stories about my birth—the excitement surrounding my arrival, the hopes and dreams my family had for me. But those stories always had a missing piece, an absence so significant it left a void in every tale: my dad. His absence loomed large over my childhood, casting a shadow that seemed to follow me everywhere. I lived in a space between questions and answers, where confusion lingered, and loneliness settled in my chest like an ache I couldn't escape.

A Fatherless Childhood

I watched other girls with their fathers—sitting on their laps, sharing jokes, being what society calls "daddy's girl." I felt like an outsider, disconnected from that kind of love, as though it was a privilege I hadn't earned. I tried to understand, but the more I observed, the more I felt adrift. People would say, "A dad is a girl's first love," but that sentiment didn't resonate with me. To me, it was a fairy tale meant for someone else.

My father's absence planted seeds of doubt in my heart—doubt about my worth, about what I deserved, and about the kind of love I could expect from the world. Those seeds grew into a tangled mess of questions without answers. Was I not enough? Why would someone abandon their child? The questions spiraled endlessly, shaping how I saw myself and how I moved through the world.

The Pain of Absence

The emptiness he left wasn't just physical; it seeped into my psyche, a silent ache I carried for years. I would lie in bed at night, staring at the ceiling, imagining what could have been. Each unanswered question became a scar, a reminder of a love that never had the chance to bloom. My father's absence left a gaping hole in me, one I would spend years trying to fill.

I watched friends' bond with their fathers over fishing trips, car rides, or even something as simple as sharing a meal. I longed for those moments, but they felt like watching a movie through a foggy window—familiar yet entirely out of reach. My father was a ghost in my life, a concept rather than a person. The confusion ran deep, and the rejection felt personal, even though I couldn't fully grasp it.

Lessons I Never Learned

A dad is supposed to teach his daughter countless lessons: how beautiful she is, how she deserves to be treated, and what to expect from the world. I never had those lessons. I didn't have a guiding hand to show me how to navigate love or relationships. The first time I experienced romantic feelings, I was lost. I didn't know what a healthy relationship looked like or how a man should treat a woman. Deep down, I longed for someone to teach me what to look for, what to avoid, and how to protect myself emotionally.

Instead, I gravitated toward relationships that mirrored my father's absence. I sought affection and approval from men who were emotionally unavailable. It was as though I was drawn to the very thing that had hurt me most, finding comfort in the familiarity of pain.

Fragile Connections

My aunt tried to bridge the gap between my father and me. Whenever I visited her, she would call him, hoping to give me a chance to hear his voice. Each time, my heart pounded—torn between the hope of connection and the certainty of disappointment. I longed to hear him yet feared the hurt that often followed. When he answered, the dam inside me would break. I'd cry uncontrollably, overwhelmed by emotions I didn't fully understand. I yearned for him but couldn't grasp why he wasn't there.

The pain was sharpest when I ran into him by chance—maybe at the grocery store or around town. Those fleeting encounters felt like cruel jokes, as though the universe was dangling a glimpse of what I could never truly have. My heart would tighten, knowing it might be months or years before I saw him again. I analyzed every detail of those moments: the way he walked, the sound of his voice, even the funny, embarrassing noise his car made in reverse. These fragments became the only pieces of him I could hold onto.

Anger and Misplaced Blame

For a long time, I directed my anger toward my mother. As a child, I needed someone to blame. Sometimes, I lashed out at her, convinced that she was the reason he was gone. I couldn't see how hard she worked to love me and provide for me, filling both parental roles. It wasn't until I became a mother myself that I understood her struggle. I found myself in a relationship with a man who treated me the way my father had treated her—distant, absent, emotionally unavailable. Only then did I grasp the depth of her sacrifices and her unwavering love for me.

Positive Role Models

I had positive male role models in my life—uncles, grandparents, and a godfather—who tried to fill the void. They treated me with respect and kindness, teaching me what I deserved from others. But they weren't my dad. No matter how much love they gave, the hole he left behind remained. It's a strange thing to miss someone who was never truly there, but I missed him all the same.

A Late Attempt to Reconnect

As I grew older, my dad began to reach out, trying to be a part of my life. But by then, the damage had been done. Years of neglect and distance had left scars that no phone call or text message could erase. His attempts to reconnect felt too late, like he was trying to fit a broken puzzle piece back into a picture that had already changed. I wanted to let him in, but the pain of feeling unwanted made it almost impossible to trust that this time would be different. So, I pushed him away, letting the walls around my heart grow thicker. It was easier to shut him out than risk the agony of abandonment again.

Then came the day he reached out through Facebook, sending a message that reopened old wounds. His apology felt hollow, as though it came from guilt rather than understanding. In that moment, I realized I didn't need him to fix the broken parts of me. I had already spent years working on that, finding my own strength and healing on my own terms.

Finding Strength in Closure

When I closed the door on him that day, it wasn't out of bitterness—it was out of strength. I no longer needed his love to feel whole. I was enough, just as I was.

The Ache of Milestones

My father's absence impacted me most during milestones: father-daughter breakfasts in elementary school, father-daughter dances in middle school, and even prom. I used to watch my friends write heartfelt social media posts about their fathers, while I secretly wrote letters to myself. On April 15, 2017, I wrote: "There are three important days a girl dreams about: her prom, her wedding day, and the day she becomes a parent. These are the days a daughter would want her dad."

When I graduated high school and didn't see him in the crowd, a part of me went numb. Over time, the piece of my heart that missed him began to wither. His absence no longer surprised me, but it still hurt.

Imagining What Could Have Been

As a child, my imagination was my escape. I would dream of what life would have been like if he had been present: trips to the park, mall outings, proudly calling him "Daddy." But those dreams were just that—dreams. Reality was different, and his absence shaped how I saw myself. I viewed myself as someone unworthy, someone no one wanted. That insecurity followed me into relationships, making me vulnerable to those who mirrored his emotional unavailability.

A Bittersweet Encounter

I'll never forget one summer day at the grocery store. My aunt, little brother, and I were shopping when my aunt called out, "Meme, look!" I turned and saw him—my dad. My heart raced as I ran to hug him. The brief exchange filled me with hope. He promised to take me to the summer fair, and I held onto that promise like it was the most precious thing in the world. But when the time came, he didn't show. My aunt called him repeatedly, and eventually, he answered, saying he would come later. By the time he arrived, we only spent twenty minutes at the fair. Still, I cherished every second, knowing it might be the last time I'd see him for a long while.

Letting Go of the Hurt

I struggled with faith and understanding God's plan for many years. I couldn't grasp why He would allow my father to abandon me. It wasn't until I became a mother that I began to see the bigger picture. When my dad resurfaced after my daughter's birth, I realized I no longer needed him to heal me. After one final message to him—telling him I could no longer allow his inconsistency to hurt me—I broke down in tears and prayed for strength. That prayer marked the beginning of my healing journey.

Through it all, I've learned that I am enough. My father's absence may have shaped my early years, but it no longer defines me. I am stronger, wiser, and whole—not because of him, but in spite of him.

CHAPTER 3:

The Betrayal of My Life

Chapter 3:
The Betrayal of My Life

Innocence Shattered

Growing up, I was surrounded by strong male figures—the kind every little girl dreams of. They were role models who inspired confidence and protection, teaching me how to ride a bike, tie my shoes, and navigate the small challenges of childhood. Their love and laughter created a world that felt secure and safe. Yet, as time passed, the warmth in their gazes was replaced by something darker, something unsettling. At the age of five, I couldn't articulate what was wrong, but deep within me, I knew: the man who was meant to protect me had become the very monster I feared.

In my innocence, I had learned to trust, to feel safe under his watchful eye. But that trust was betrayed in the most devastating way. His transformation was subtle, insidious. To my family, he remained charming—smiling, laughing, and playing his role flawlessly. Beneath the facade, however, lurked a predator. At five years old, I didn't have the words to describe what was happening to me. What had once been a safe touch morphed into something that made me want to scream, but the screams never came. Instead, they were swallowed by fear, festering silently within me.

A Child's Silent Pain

I was just a child, still learning to make sense of the world. Yet, I was forced to endure horrors no child should ever face. My cries for help grew quieter with each passing day, and though tears often came, they brought no relief. Each tear felt like fire, leaving behind a hollow ache that words couldn't soothe. Over time, even my tears dried up, leaving me drowning in silence.

Each night, I lay in bed, tormented by one question: Why is this happening to me? I pleaded with God for answers, questioning my worth and searching for reasons why I deserved such a fate. The betrayal by someone my family trusted left me feeling isolated, abandoned, and unworthy of love. Nights became an endless cycle of dread. My body, transformed by trauma, woke me at precisely 4 a.m. each morning—not in relief, but in terror. Sleep offered no escape; it only brought nightmares.

Living in Fear

The terror always began with a sound: slow, deliberate footsteps echoing down the hallway. The anticipation of those footsteps sent my body into shock—my breath hitched, and my heart raced, threatening to burst from my chest. I knew what was coming long before the door opened, but that knowledge brought no comfort, only dread. The instinct to curl inward, to protect myself, was futile; his hands were always stronger.

In those moments, I screamed louder than I thought possible, begging him to stop, praying for someone— anyone—to hear me. But no one ever came. The isolation deepened, and I felt trapped in an endless nightmare.

The Burden of Silence

I longed to share my truth, to shout it from the rooftops, but fear silenced me. His words echoed relentlessly in my mind: "If you tell, you'll break the heart of someone who carries yours." The guilt of potentially shattering my family weighed heavier than my own suffering. I convinced myself that silence was the only way to protect the people I loved, even as it slowly consumed me.

The pain I endured wasn't just physical. It sank deeper, transforming into emotional and mental wounds that grew with time. Starting at five years old and lasting through my teenage years, it felt as though I had lived a lifetime of suffering. By the time I was twelve, I thought like a seventeen-year-old. By seventeen, I carried the weight of a twenty-one-year-old's heartbreak. The innocence that should have been mine was stolen by someone I had once trusted implicitly.

The Betrayal Revealed

By the age of twenty-one, the burden of my pain became unbearable. The secret I had carried for so long was suffocating me. One night, desperate for relief, I confided in my boyfriend. I hoped sharing my burden would ease the weight, but his reaction shattered me further. In a moment of anger, he exposed my deepest secret on social media, laying bare the pain I had hidden for so long. That night, it felt as if the ground beneath me had crumbled, leaving me in free fall. For the first time, I believed there was no way back.

The day I had always dreaded finally arrived: my mother and some of my family learned the truth. The weight of my decision to stay silent came crashing down as I witnessed their devastation. Some cried, broken by the reality I had worked so hard to shield them from. Watching the people I loved crumble under the weight of my truth mirrored my own pain, amplifying the sorrow that already consumed me.

The Guilt of Speaking Out

I thought that finally speaking my truth would bring relief, but instead, I felt overwhelming guilt. As the words left my mouth, I didn't feel lighter—I felt like I had done something wrong. A knot formed in my stomach, and I wanted to disappear. Seeing the shock and heartbreak on my mother's face felt like the ultimate betrayal. She had always tried to protect me, and I felt as though I had shattered her world.

I had expected relief, but instead, I felt like I had ruined everything. The questions I had dreaded came flooding in—questions I wasn't ready to answer. I didn't want to relive the dark places I had worked so hard to bury, but I knew, as soon as I spoke, that this moment would never end. It was just the beginning of something I could never take back.

Fragments of the Past

I remember being six or seven, just finishing playing outside with the neighbors, when he would say little things like, "Let me take a picture of you right now and set it as my screensaver." I didn't think anything of it and smiled for the photo. It became worse when I'd take a bath and find him standing in the doorway, watching. I'd try to hide behind the shower curtain, but his presence felt inescapable. "If you tell, the people will be very disappointed and will hurt me so bad. Do you want to see me hurt?" he would say. His manipulation was like an anchor dragging me deeper into silence.

Each time it got worse. It often happened when I was sleeping. He'd wake me, sliding me to the edge of the bed. I'd scream, cry, and kick, but his strength overpowered me. "You're raping me," I'd yell. "I can't rape you," he'd reply. "Only people your age can." His words echoed in my mind, filling me with despair. After each incident, I'd run to the closet, crying myself to sleep, waiting for someone to come home.

The Toll of Trauma

The constant fear and trauma took a toll on my mental health. At four in the morning, I'd wake up, shaking and crying uncontrollably. My mom, unaware of what I was going through, took me to the doctor, who diagnosed me with anxiety and depression. As much as I wanted to tell someone, I couldn't. His words, his threats, kept me silent.

Finding a Way to Heal

As a teenager, I began to open up to people I trusted, like my best friend and boyfriend. But I always made them swear to keep my secret. I turned away from God, questioning how He could allow me to endure so much pain at such a young age. Yet, despite my anger, I still went to church every Sunday, searching for answers.

At the age of twenty, I decided I wanted to heal. I started Googling ways to move forward, but nothing seemed to help. Then, I heard God's voice guiding me:

1. Handle the trauma by showing yourself sympathy.
2. Confront and process your emotions.
3. Understand what you're feeling.
4. Forgive.
5. Wait for your new beginning.

Each step was a battle, but slowly, I began to find peace. Though the journey to healing continues, I now know that my trauma does not define me. My strength, resilience, and faith are what make me who I am.

"I longed to share my truth, to shout it from the rooftops, but fear silenced me. His words echoed relentlessly in my mind: 'If you tell, you'll break the heart of someone who carries yours.' The guilt of potentially shattering my family weighed heavier than my own suffering."

~Myasia White

CHAPTER 4:
The Illusion

Chapter 4:
The Illusion

The Promise of Forever

When I met him at 17, I thought I had found the answer
to all my prayers. After all the pain and trauma I had
endured growing up, I believed he was my escape. He
seemed like a dream, the perfect picture of love, like the
kind you see in 90s movies. We talked about the future as
if we were already living in it. We were supposed to get
married, have kids, and grow old together. It was that
"forever" love—the kind that sweeps you off your feet
and makes you believe in happily-ever-afters. For a
moment, I thought I was living it.

Cracks in the Fairytale

In the beginning, he was everything I had ever wanted. He
said all the right things, painting a picture of a life that felt
too good to be true. He adored me—or at least that's what
he told me. Every moment with him felt like a scene from
a fairytale. I clung to every word, every promise, every
dream he spun like a web. I was young and hopeful, ready
to believe in the magic of us. But what I thought was love
was only the bait. Slowly, little cracks began to show.

At first, the cracks were barely noticeable—the offhand comments, the subtle digs. He'd tell me I was "too sensitive" when I got upset, brushing off my feelings as if they were nothing. The first time he called me "stupid," it felt like a punch to the gut. He apologized, of course, claiming he was just frustrated, and I believed him. I convinced myself it was no big deal. Everyone says things they don't mean in the heat of the moment, right? But that was just the beginning. Over time, his words cut deeper: "fat," "worthless," "pathetic." Insults became a regular part of our lives.

Manipulation and Control

It wasn't just the name-calling. He turned everything into my fault. If he was in a bad mood, it was because I didn't make him happy. If he cheated, it was because I wasn't good enough. He made me believe I was always the problem, and I carried that blame like a weight on my shoulders. The worst part wasn't just how he treated me but how he made me question myself. His manipulation crept into my mind like poison until I couldn't even recognize the person staring back at me in the mirror.

The abuse wasn't always physical, but when it was, I blamed myself for that too. I convinced myself that I provoked him, that if I had done something differently, it wouldn't have happened. And when I cried, he'd tell me I was weak, that I was "too much." Somehow, in that twisted reality, I believed him. Every time he left, I waited for him to come back, clinging to the hope that he'd change.

A Prison of Fear

By June 2017, I was pregnant. The life growing inside me should have been a beacon of hope, but instead, it felt like a prison sentence. I hated who I had become—broken, weak, unrecognizable. I was carrying the child of a man who had ripped apart my soul, and I couldn't see a way out.

When my baby was six months old, I had to work a short shift. I asked him to watch her, and to my surprise, he agreed. He showed up at my job with his friend to pick her up. Relief washed over me. I thought, *Maybe he's finally stepping up.* But that relief quickly turned into a nightmare.

The Nightmare Unfolds

After my shift, I called him to get my baby back, and he didn't answer. The calls kept going to voicemail. Panic set in as I tried again and again—five, six, seven times, each unanswered call tightening the knot in my stomach. I stayed with a friend that night, desperate to hide my fear from my family, knowing they would only blame me for trusting him.

I finally reached out to his friend, hoping for answers. To my surprise, his friend gave me an address. But when I got there, chaos spiraled further. He came to my car drunk, slurring his words, and insisted my baby wasn't there. I couldn't believe it. His friend, who seemed to pity me, confessed that I deserved better. Then, he tried to force himself on me.

Terror and rage exploded inside me. I fought back with everything I had, throwing my car into reverse and speeding off, not caring what I hit. I called my best friend, screaming, crying, desperate to find my baby. I reached out to his family, the police, anyone who might help. But no one could. They all said the same thing—he was her father, and I couldn't do anything.

A Mother's Desperation

For 24 hours, I lived a nightmare, wondering where my child was and if she was safe. Finally, he texted me a picture of her, as if it was some cruel game. Hours later, he told me where to meet him. When I saw her, my heart broke and healed at the same time. I held her close, vowing never to let this happen again.

But it didn't end there. He used every opportunity to create chaos, stirring drama between me and his girlfriend. He thrived on the pain and destruction he caused, bouncing from one household to another, leaving a trail of heartbreak in his wake. For years, I let him control my life, my emotions, and my self-worth.

The Final Betrayal

The breaking point came when I realized he didn't just hurt me—he tried to destroy me. In April 2020, he humiliated me in a way I never thought possible. He took the most vulnerable part of my story and turned it into a weapon for the world to see. He blasted me on social media, revealing the darkest secret I had shared with him in confidence. A secret I had carried silently for years became a spectacle.

The shame hit me first, then the anger. I confronted him, trembling with hurt and fury, but his response was cold and dismissive. "I'll delete it. Everyone didn't see it," he said, shrugging off my pain like it was nothing. There was no apology, no remorse, no understanding of the depth of what he had done.

Finding Freedom

By April 2020, something shifted. I was numb. His words, his actions, his very presence—all of it disgusted me. I was done. Not in the half-hearted way I had been before, but truly, finally done. Looking back, that day was a blessing in disguise. He thought he was destroying me, but he was setting me free. That moment of ultimate betrayal forced me to confront the truth I had been too scared to face: there was no saving us. There was no saving him. The only way I could save myself was by walking away for good.

Lessons Learned

I clung to the illusion that he could change—that the love we shared was stronger than the hurt. I believed he was the answer to all my prayers, a fairytale escape from the pain and trauma I had endured growing up. His promises of forever, of marriage, children, and a life of love, felt like a dream come true. But the illusion began to shatter as his true self emerged.

His insults, manipulation, and gaslighting made me question my worth. I blamed myself for everything, convinced that if I were better, he would treat me better. My confidence and self-worth were shattered. But through the pain, I learned that no one can define my worth except me. Walking away was the hardest thing I've ever done, but it was also the bravest.

The illusion he created may have broken me for a time, but in the end, it gave me the strength to rebuild myself. And for that, I am grateful.

"I clung to every word, every promise, every dream he spun like a web. I was young and hopeful, ready to believe in the magic of us. But what I thought was love was only the bait."

~Myasia White

CHAPTER 5:

Embracing Unplanned Paths

Chapter 5:
Embracing Unplanned Paths

Dreams of Perfection

As a young girl, I dreamed of a picture-perfect life. My aspirations were simple yet profound: graduate from college, establish a career, marry my soulmate, live in a cozy house with a white picket fence, a dog running in the yard, and laughter filling the air. I envisioned a life where everything fell into place seamlessly. It was a vision society often celebrates—a life of happiness and stability. With high hopes and big dreams, the perfect family felt like the natural progression for me.

The Unexpected Reality

But life rarely unfolds the way we imagine. At just 18, I found myself facing the unexpected reality of impending motherhood. It began one seemingly ordinary day while I was working at an after-school care program. I felt an unusual sensation—something just felt off. As I shared my discomfort with a friend and coworker, she looked at me and asked a question that would change everything: "Are you late on your cycle?"

At first, I laughed it off, convinced there was no way that could be true. But when I checked my cycle tracker, the realization hit me like a thunderbolt: I was late. My heart raced as the weight of my situation began to settle on my shoulders. I shared my discovery with my friend, who immediately insisted we get a pregnancy test.

Two Red Lines

Taking the test was surreal. As I watched the lines form, a mix of anticipation and dread consumed me. When those two red lines appeared, I couldn't believe my eyes. I was only 18, freshly graduated from high school, without a job or a plan. The dreams I had so meticulously crafted seemed to crumble in an instant. It was difficult to accept that I could only blame myself for the situation I found myself in.

When it came time to tell my child's father, I was filled with a strange mixture of hope and fear. To my surprise, he responded with overwhelming joy, exclaiming that he would tell his family the news. But the heaviest burden remained: breaking the news to my mother. It was the conversation I had dreaded most, and it felt monumental.

Breaking the News

I struggled to find the right words, sensing deep down that my mother already had an inkling of what was happening. One day, without warning, she asked me to take a pregnancy test in front of her. Panicking, I intentionally missed the stick, hoping to shield her from the inevitable heartbreak. When the test came back negative, I knew I couldn't hide the truth any longer. Summoning all my courage, I finally told her the result was positive.

The disappointment on her face was crushing. The weight of my choices bore down on me, and I couldn't shake the feeling that I had let her down. The very next week, I had my first doctor's appointment to confirm the pregnancy. As the sonographer performed the ultrasound, I braced myself for the unknown. Then, the words came: "Congratulations, there's the baby." My due date was set for February 14, 2018.

Isolation and Betrayal

Mixed emotions flooded my heart. On one hand, I felt the joy of bringing a new life into the world. On the other, I was engulfed by fear and uncertainty. As time passed, the reality of my situation began to sink in. Friends I thought would stand by me started to fade away, and the support system I had imagined dwindled. As my pregnancy became more visible, a cascade of emotions overwhelmed me.

The child's father, who had once been so enthusiastic, began cheating more frequently and grew increasingly spiteful. Consumed by his own family issues, he left me feeling abandoned and forgotten. It was devastating to watch someone who once celebrated this new chapter with me now treat me like an afterthought. My pregnancy became a traumatizing experience, overshadowed by betrayal and neglect. Thankfully, my mother and sister were unwavering in their support. Though my mother was initially disappointed, she never left my side. She ensured I had everything I needed, even if it meant sacrificing her own comfort.

The Birth of My Daughter

As my due date approached, the hospital became a second home. My blood pressure skyrocketed, and I faced multiple instances of preterm labor. The stress weighed heavily on me, manifesting physically and emotionally. On January 27, 2018, I attended my great-grandmother's birthday party, hoping for a moment of joy. But after eating a piece of fish, contractions began. Initially, I dismissed them as Braxton Hicks, but as the days passed, the contractions worsened.

Finally, I sought medical help. My OB-GYN advised that I should be admitted to the hospital because I was in active labor. Arriving at the hospital at 5 PM, I was immediately hooked up to IVs and closely monitored. Despite their efforts, I wasn't dilating, and the doctors ultimately scheduled a C-section. Tears streamed down my face as the reality of my first surgery sank in.

On January 30, 2018, at 12:45 PM, I welcomed a beautiful baby girl into the world. The moment I laid eyes on her, love flooded my heart. Yet amidst that joy, I felt an unsettling disconnect. I struggled to bond with my daughter, caught in a whirlwind of conflicting emotions. Happiness and fear intertwined, making it difficult to grasp the depth of my feelings.

Postpartum Depression

As the weeks passed, I grappled with an overwhelming array of emotions. I felt isolated and unable to connect with my own child. Each time she cried, I found myself crying too, trapped in a cycle of despair. I was suffering in silence, unaware of the extent of my struggles. After six weeks, my doctor diagnosed me with postpartum depression. Hearing those words was terrifying and liberating all at once. I wasn't alone in my suffering—I had a name for it.

With my mother and sister's unwavering support, I began navigating the complexities of motherhood while battling depression. They cared for my baby when I needed moments to myself. Still, judgment from others deepened my feelings of inadequacy. Comments comparing me to my mother made me feel like I was failing. I often felt like I was drowning in a sea of expectations, struggling just to stay afloat.

Bonding Through Love

One question haunted me constantly: How can I protect a person when I couldn't even protect myself as a kid? That realization was a heavy burden to bear. There were days when I felt like everything was falling apart. I'd ask my mom to watch the baby so I could retreat to a quiet room and break down. I needed to cry, to scream, to release the weight of it all.

Bonding with my baby didn't come naturally. Every attempt felt forced, and the love I thought I should feel seemed distant. Guilt consumed me. I desperately wanted someone to understand that I was doing my best, even if my best didn't look the way I thought it should.

It wasn't until four months after her birth that I truly began to bond with my daughter. One day, as she smiled and made sweet baby noises, something shifted. I realized my love for her had been there all along, buried beneath the weight of my pain. From that moment on, she became the light in my darkest days. She made me feel like her superhero, even though she was the one saving me.

Lessons from the Journey

Through this journey, I've learned valuable lessons about resilience, love, and self-acceptance. Motherhood is not an easy journey, but it's worth every step we take.

For those who know someone suffering from postpartum depression, offering support is crucial. Let them know they aren't alone, that they are capable of overcoming anything, and that it's okay to seek help.

Tips for Navigating Postpartum Depression

1. **Believe in Yourself:** Trust your strength and capability to raise your child.
2. **Seek Support:** Reach out to family, friends, or support groups for encouragement.
3. **Take Time for Yourself:** Prioritize your mental and emotional well-being.
4. **Focus on Healing:** Address past traumas to become the best parent you can be.
5. **Set Goals:** Work toward achievable goals to provide direction and hope.
6. **Celebrate Small Victories:** Every step forward, no matter how small, is progress.
7. **Create a Positive Environment:** Build a loving, supportive home for yourself and your child.

You are your own village. Trust your journey and remember that every twist and turn shapes the narrative of your life.

CHAPTER 6:

Bent But Not Broken

Chapter 6:
Bent But Not Broken

The Weight of the Past

After everything was said and done, the weight of my past felt like a mountain crushing my soul. Each breath came with the heaviness of a life shaped by trauma, and every step was slowed by the chains of a history I couldn't escape. The burden of molestation loomed over me like a suffocating shadow, a constant reminder of a stolen childhood—of innocence ripped away too soon. The scars were invisible but ran deep, making it hard to trust, to feel safe, or to believe that love wasn't inherently painful.

A Void That Couldn't Be Filled

Growing up without a father left a void so wide that I tried to fill it with anything that might offer the warmth and safety I craved. But no matter how hard I tried, relationships didn't heal the emptiness. Instead, they often magnified my wounds. Each failed attempt at love and every betrayal seemed to confirm what I had feared all along: that I was unworthy of care, that I was somehow broken.

My last relationship was the worst of all—a whirlwind of manipulation, emotional abuse, and lies that left me shattered. My partner's narcissism gnawed away at my self-worth until I could barely recognize myself. My heart was torn apart, and my confidence was in ruins. The aftermath of that relationship felt like the final straw. I was left to pick up the pieces of my broken heart while shouldering the heavy responsibility of being a single mother. It wasn't just my pain I had to carry—I had to be strong for my daughter, to protect her from the very storms that were threatening to drown me.

The Mask of Strength

On the outside, I appeared to be a tower of strength—the devoted mother who always had a smile, the woman who seemed to have it all together. I wore my strength like armor, hiding behind it as though it could shield me from the truth. People admired me, even envied me, but they didn't know that behind the mask, I was slowly crumbling. The pain was too deep, the weight too heavy to bear alone, but admitting that felt like failure. So, I kept the mask on, pretending I was fine, that I was invincible. But it was a lie, and I was suffocating under the pressure.

Triggers and Pain

It didn't take much to unravel me—a certain smell in the air, the sound of a particular song on the radio, or a passing comment that struck too close to home. These tiny, seemingly insignificant moments pulled me back into places I had long tried to forget, dragging me into a whirlwind of painful memories. I would feel the tears welling up at the most unexpected times, but I had trained myself to hold them in. My cries were silent, reserved for moments when no one could see. They came in the shower, where the water could disguise my tears, though it never washed away the ache in my heart. Hiding from the storm felt impossible when the storm lived inside me.

The Lowest Point

At night, I would lie awake, staring at the ceiling and wondering, *Why am I so bad at this thing called life?* The question haunted me as I tried to understand why happiness seemed so elusive, why everything felt so hard. I started to believe I was cursed, that God had placed me in an endless cycle of hurt and unhappiness with no way out. Some days, I couldn't even bring myself to get out of bed. The weight of depression made the very thought of facing the world unbearable. The pain of my past consumed me, and I began to wonder if life would be easier without me in it. I started making plans—plans that I believed would end the torment and bring peace. Or so I thought.

April 11, 2020: A Day to Remember

I remember the day vividly. The cold, hard bathroom floor pressed against my skin as my body shook with sobs that wouldn't stop. It felt like my heart had shattered into a million pieces, and I was drowning in darkness. I had convinced myself that my daughter would be better off without me, that she would be cared for, and that was all that mattered. At that moment, I was ready to surrender. Ready to let go of the pain. Ready to stop fighting.

In my desperation, I reached for my phone. My hands trembled as I dialed my mother's number. When she answered, I whispered the words I had been too afraid to say before: "I can't do this anymore."

A Mother's Love

She came immediately. When she walked into my apartment, her eyes were wide with panic, but she didn't hesitate. She wrapped me in her arms and held me tight as I cried. Through my sobs, she whispered words of love and encouragement, telling me that I couldn't give up, that I had to keep fighting. And in that moment, something shifted inside me.

Finding Faith

I had always heard people say that God meets you when you are at your lowest, and for the first time, I understood what they meant. It was as if God was there, whispering, "Myasia, you've got this. Just because you're in the storm doesn't mean I'm not right beside you, holding the umbrella. Trust me; this will become part of your testimony."

Choosing to Heal

In the days that followed, I made a decision—a choice that felt like the hardest thing I'd ever done. I chose to trust. I chose to believe there was a way out of the darkness, even if I couldn't see it yet. My mother, always my rock, encouraged me to seek therapy. Though I was terrified of facing my pain and uncovering the truths I had buried deep within, I knew I couldn't keep carrying this burden alone.

The Journey of Rediscovery

The first few therapy sessions were excruciating. It felt like being ripped open, forced to relive the pain I had spent years suppressing. But little by little, the weight began to lift. For the first time, I had someone who could help me untangle my thoughts, someone who could guide me out of the chaos and toward the light.

The journey wasn't just about healing from the past—it was about rediscovering who I was. For so long, I had been lost in the pain, in the roles I had to play, in the masks I wore to protect myself. I didn't recognize who I had become. It felt like I was on a first date with myself, asking questions I had long forgotten to ask: *What's your favorite color? What makes you laugh? What brings you to tears?* I had to learn who I was all over again, peeling back layers of trauma to uncover the real me.

Forgiveness and Faith

In that process of self-discovery, I realized something powerful—I wouldn't trade my journey for anything. As painful as it had been, it had shaped me. Yes, it had scarred me, but it had also made me stronger in ways I was only beginning to understand. It all came back to what my mom had always said: "You have a purpose, even if you don't know what it is yet."

One afternoon before a therapy session, I felt a quiet whisper urging me to explore the idea of forgiveness. It was as if God was saying, "If you learn to forgive, you'll finally be able to let go of the pain and find peace." A Bible verse echoed in my mind: "Seek first the kingdom of heaven, and everything will be added unto you." I clung to that verse, believing healing was within reach.

Forgiveness wasn't easy. It wasn't something I could simply decide to do. But I worked diligently, step by step, and as I did, the chains that had bound me to my past began to loosen. Slowly but surely, the weight lifted, and I started to feel lighter.

Thriving, Not Just Surviving

Some days, the shadows still creep in. The weight of the past still threatens to pull me under. But I've learned to meet those feelings with compassion. I've learned to heal the little girl within me, comforting her when she feels afraid. I remind myself of how far I've come, of the battles I've fought and won.

I'm no longer just surviving. I'm thriving. The fears that once paralyzed me have been replaced with courage, and the doubts have been silenced by a deep faith that I am exactly where I am meant to be. Today, I embrace my past as a testament to my strength, a story of survival and growth. I am a fighter, a survivor, and a woman who has turned her pain into power.

"I had always heard people say that God meets you when you are at your lowest, and for the first time, I understood what they meant. It was as if God was there, whispering, 'You've got this. Just because you're in the storm doesn't mean I'm not right beside you, holding the umbrella.'"

~Myasia White

CHAPTER 7:

A Mess into a Message

Chapter 7:
A Mess into a Message

Finding Light in the Darkness

Life has a way of presenting storms that feel endless and trials that seem insurmountable. I've been there—deep in what felt like unending darkness, struggling to find light and purpose. But God has a way of bringing beauty out of brokenness—transforming messes into messages and tests into testimonies. Through every struggle, He reveals His faithfulness, mercy, and love, even when we can't yet see the bigger picture.

A Day That Changed Everything

For me, the turning point came on June 20, 2020—a day that changed my life forever. It was the day I rededicated my life to Christ and was baptized. That experience felt like being born again in every sense of the word. The crushing weight on my soul lifted, and for the first time, I understood what it meant to be truly free. Washed clean, I stepped into a new life, a renewed spirit, and a deeper trust in God's purpose for my life—even when I didn't fully understand it.

Recognizing God's Presence

In the months that followed, I began to recognize how God had been working in my life all along, even in ways I hadn't yet realized. Isaiah 65:24 says, "Before they call I will answer; while they are still speaking, I will hear." Even before I called out to Him, He was orchestrating moments of healing, placing people and opportunities in my path to meet needs I hadn't even acknowledged.

The Gift of the Williams Family

One of the most profound examples of God's provision came on May 1, 2021, when I met the Williams family. At the time, my heart was worn from past hurts, and I had been praying for a kind of love and support I'd never truly experienced. I longed for someone who wouldn't hurt or disappoint me—a person who could show me healthy, unconditional love. Little did I know, God was already working behind the scenes.

The Williams family was an answer to a prayer I hadn't even fully known how to ask. From the moment we met, they welcomed my daughter and me with open arms. Their warmth, acceptance, and unwavering love felt like a glimpse of heaven on earth. They weren't just friends— they became family, a support system unlike anything I had ever known. For the first time, I experienced what "perfect family love" felt like, and every time I reflect on their impact, I'm overwhelmed with gratitude. Through them, God showed me that His love is often reflected in the people He places in our lives at just the right time.

Restoring Broken Relationships

Another remarkable chapter in my journey was the restoration of my relationship with my biological father. For years, resentment and past wounds kept us apart. But as I drew closer to God, He began to heal my heart. I prayed not just for my own healing, but for the relationship I thought was beyond repair. Over time, God softened both of our hearts, opening doors for communication and reconciliation. Piece by piece, He rebuilt what had been broken, reminding me that nothing is impossible with Him.

The Power of Forgiveness

Forgiveness played a significant role in this restoration, as it did in so many areas of my healing. It wasn't easy—confronting deep pain and letting go of long-held anger never is. But forgiveness was the key to unlocking a new perspective on life. When I finally chose to forgive, my world began to transform. I experienced a freedom I hadn't known before, and my outlook on life shifted.

Facing the Darkest Moments

The journey wasn't without its challenges. Healing meant facing the darkest parts of my past, including moments of despair that brought me to my knees. I'll never forget April 11, 2020—a day when I reached my breaking point. The pain felt insurmountable, and I was ready to give up. But in my darkest moment, God's voice broke through the chaos, whispering to me that my story wasn't over. "Just because you're in the storm," He seemed to say, "doesn't mean I'm not right beside you, holding the umbrella."

Choosing to Fight

From that day forward, I chose to fight—for my daughter, for myself, and for the future God promised me. Therapy became a crucial part of my healing journey. Though difficult at first, it helped me untangle the pain and confusion that had built up over the years. Slowly, I began to see glimpses of light breaking through the darkness.

God continued to remind me of His promises, especially through verses like Isaiah 40:31: "But they who wait for the Lord shall renew their strength; they shall mount up with wings like eagles; they shall run and not be weary; they shall walk and not faint." These words carried me through the hardest days, reminding me that God's strength is made perfect in our weakness.

Gratitude and Healing

I also found healing through gratitude. Journaling became a daily practice, helping me focus on the small blessings— my daughter's laughter, the kindness of a friend, the beauty of a sunrise. Each moment of gratitude brought me closer to the realization that God's goodness was all around me, even amidst the struggles.

Turning Pain Into Purpose

Looking back, I can see how every trial served a purpose. The storms taught me resilience, patience, and faith. They prepared me for the blessings I now cherish and gave me a story to share with others. Jeremiah 29:11 has been a constant source of encouragement: "For I know the plans I have for you," declares the Lord, "plans to prosper you and not to harm you, plans to give you hope and a future."

A Message of Hope

Today, I stand in awe of God's faithfulness. The relationships He's restored, the love He's provided, and the strength He's given me are all reminders that He is a God of redemption. He takes our mess and turns it into a masterpiece.

To anyone facing their own storm, I want to say this: God sees you. He hears your cries and knows your pain. Trust that He is working behind the scenes, orchestrating something beautiful. Let your struggles refine you, your trials strengthen you, and your journey inspire others.

Let your mess become a message. Let your test become a testimony. God is turning your struggles into something beautiful, and brighter days are just ahead.

CHAPTER 8:

Beyond Strength

Chapter 8:
Beyond Strength

Reflecting on the Journey

At 26 years old, I reflect on my life and acknowledge the many obstacles I've faced. Each one has been a steppingstone on my path to becoming who I am today. It hasn't always been easy, but through every trial, I've come to understand the depth of my strength and the power of my faith. I'm not perfect, and I don't claim to be. But I stand here, grounded in an ongoing relationship with God, who is the head of my life, guiding me through every twist and turn.

One of my greatest blessings is my daughter, Madison. Now seven years old, she is the highlight of my day and the light in my life. Every moment spent with her reminds me why I fight through challenges. Her laughter fills my heart with joy, and her curiosity inspires me to strive for more. I want to show her that it's okay to stumble; what matters is how we rise.

Becoming a Voice for the Unheard

In my journey, I've become a voice for those who feel scared or unheard. I stand for the ones who have been told, "You can't," to remind them, "YOU GOT THIS." Each of us has a unique story, and it's essential to lift each other up, especially those weighed down by doubt. I know firsthand the sting of negativity and how it can cloud your vision. But I've learned that our voices can be powerful tools for change.

Leaning Into Faith

With God's guidance, I found the strength to rise above the noise. I've faced situations that tested my resolve— moments when I questioned my abilities, my worth, and my path. Yet, through every hurdle, I leaned into my faith. I prayed for clarity, for strength, and for direction. God ordered my steps, and slowly, I began to see that my struggles could be transformed into something beautiful.

This realization fueled my desire to write *Beyond Strength: Healing Within God*. This book and journal is not just a collection of my thoughts; it is a testament to the healing power of faith. It is for anyone who has faced trauma or feels lost in their journey. I poured my heart into every page, hoping to provide comfort and encouragement to those who read it. My prayer is that they find the courage to confront their pain and recognize their own strength.

Celebrating Vulnerability

In sharing my story, I aim to create a space where vulnerability is celebrated. Healing is not linear; it's messy and complicated, but it's also beautiful. I want my readers to know that they are not alone. Each chapter of my life has brought me closer to understanding that we are all in this together, and we can lift one another as we navigate our journeys.

The Meaning of "Beyond Strength"

To me, "beyond strength" is not just enduring the pain but growing through it and finding purpose on the other side. It's about transcending the survival mindset and stepping into a space of healing, transformation, and thriving. This understanding didn't come all at once but through the accumulation of life's trials and a pivotal realization: true strength is not found in holding it all together but in allowing yourself to heal and rise.

Finding Resilience in Surrender

One moment that crystallized this for me was in April 2020, when my deepest pain became public, and I was left feeling broken and exposed. In that moment, I realized that strength was not about putting on a brave face but about surrendering to God and letting Him guide me to a place of restoration. It was through this surrender that I found my true resilience—a strength that went beyond my own abilities.

Growth Through Struggles

- **Emotional Growth:** "Beyond strength" means recognizing that we are not defined by our struggles but by how we grow through them. Emotionally, it required me to confront my pain and acknowledge the parts of myself I had buried.
- **Spiritual Growth:** Spiritually, it meant deepening my relationship with God, trusting Him to lead me through the darkness.
- **Mental Growth:** Mentally, it required shifting my perspective from a victim mentality to one of empowerment and purpose.

Anchored by Love and Faith

I discovered an unexpected source of strength in my daughter, Madison. Her laughter, curiosity, and love remind me daily why I keep going. She is my anchor and my inspiration to strive for more. I also found strength in my faith, which has been my constant foundation, and in sharing my story to help others. Each time I open up, I am reminded that vulnerability can be a source of empowerment.

Purpose Through Writing

One pivotal experience that embodies "beyond strength" was when I decided to write *Beyond Strength: Healing Within God*. This was a moment of stepping into a greater purpose, fueled by the desire to help others find healing. I poured my heart into this book, knowing that sharing my pain and triumphs could inspire someone else to rise. The process was both challenging and healing, pushing me past my limits and reminding me that my story has value.

Dreaming Bigger

Embracing "beyond strength" has allowed me to dream bigger and pursue goals I once thought impossible. I envision a future filled with purpose, where I continue to inspire others through my words, my actions, and my faith. I dream of expanding my platform, creating more opportunities to uplift others, and building a legacy that my daughter can be proud of.

Remember, you are not alone in your journey. With faith, resilience, and love, you can rise above any challenge and step into the fullness of who you were created to be.

Oh yeah, let me reintroduce myself:

My name is Myasia.
I am a survivor.
I am a warrior.
I am me.

UNBREAKABLE
BENT BUT NOT BROKEN!

MYASIA WHITE

ABOUT THE AUTHOR
MYASIA WHITE

ABOUT THE AUTHOR
MYASIA WHITE

Myasia is a survivor, a warrior, and a voice for the voiceless. As an author, speaker, and advocate for healing, she uses her personal journey to inspire others to find strength through faith. Overcoming childhood trauma, heartbreak, and self-doubt, she has dedicated her life to helping others turn their pain into purpose.

Through her writing and speaking, Myasia empowers individuals to embrace their healing journey, deepen their faith, and step into the fullness of who they were created to be. Her book, *Unbreakable: Bent But Not Broken!* is a testament to resilience, transformation, and the power of God's grace.

When she's not sharing her message of hope, Myasia is a devoted mother to her daughter, Madison, who continues to be her greatest source of inspiration.

UNBREAKABLE
BENT BUT NOT BROKEN!

MYASIA WHITE

Made in United States
Cleveland, OH
23 May 2025

17185132R10042